Deep has called

Precious Ozems

raedable

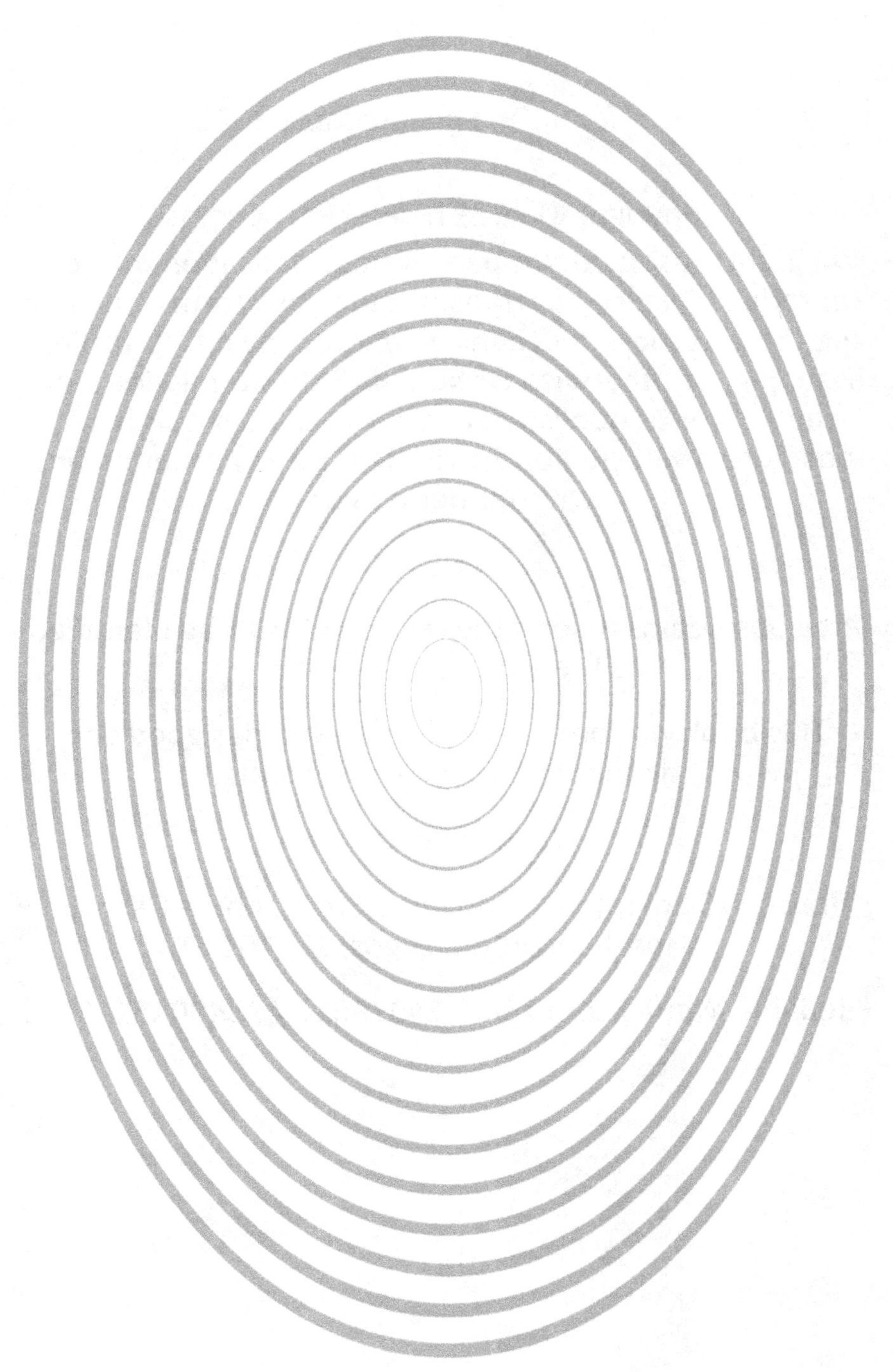

First Published by Raedable 2021



This book was professionally typeset, designed and distributed online by Raedable.

Raedable

House 3/5 Solomon Onafowope Street Abule Oshorun Ibeshe Ikorodu, Lagos, 104101

Raedable@gmail.com 2348124935612 / 2349018196749

# CONTENTS

# Dedication

Long was the night, to the ONE who made me see the day being the path in the way,

To the one whose words where my stay being the comfort till time came.

# Acknowledgments

I want to specially thank my man of God, Pastor Chris Oyakhilome, for the years of impact in my Spirit, giving my life a meaning.

I want to thank my Pastor, mother and boss, Pastor Eunice Oyeyemi for the opportunity to serve and learn first-hand kingdom principles. I also want to thank Pastor Peter Oyeyemi for his words of encouragement, they keep me going.

I want to thank an awe- inspiring personality, the president of the Loveworldnext, Daysman Oyakhilome Woghiren for your many impacts in my life.

Thank you Mr David Ehigie, you are the best...

# Papa

The only epistle I ever want to write,

is the one of you.

This is how I will start,

"I Love You",

I think it's the first thing everyone should know, My love
for you.

Let's continue;

In time I have seen how amazing you are,

this description is nothing compared

to the who you really are.

I'm still on that journey I told you about,

You remember don't you?

The journey of words.

I must find every word that would express the
magnanimity clause of your being.

So I will try this again,

In time I have seen how supernaturally

glorious you are,

touching any you meet,

in a way I would call healing.

Like you understand every fibre of the being,

So you bring the calm because you touch "the place".

You do understand, don't you?

My epistle,

So I met you and worlds turned.

Well my world did,

Yes! My world did.

There is so much to say,

but I will share this much;

I, New.

A new being, having never existed before.

I gained the identity of a family,

The gold family.

And my most perfect gift is you.

You as my Papa.

Knowing you has been the most intimate process for me,

I met me, another perfect gift.

To see and be the who I was born to be,

Perfect.

"I love you"..

My writing ink wouldn't stop;

What way would it be,

To express me giving all?

Papa deserves best,

Let me ask Thanksgiving.

"Thanksgiving" will you be enough?

"Thanksgiving" I ask again, will you be enough?

Enough to serenade my Papa's presence,

and bring him such joy that I produced.

Let me ask Papa's Candle,

Since it has the ability to search out from the belly every depth.

Candle, will you thoroughly show the deep in my within?

Let Papa see, Let Papa know,

His the One I Love.

Can I say this again,

I Love you.

My biggest would be that my words are inscribed in your heart and you read each time your heart is in search for

'the one' whose only ability is in loving you.

I Love you.

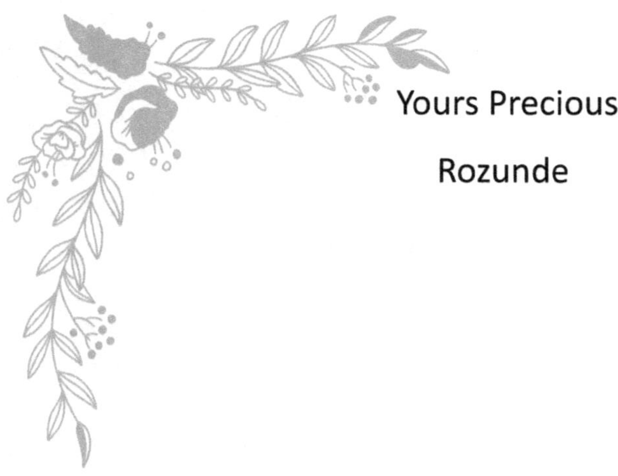

## Yours Precious

Rozunde

# 1

# *Purpose Calls*

Purpose calls,

He says my name is Christ,

I'm the path you must choose,

I'm the way you must follow,

I'm the one you are to love.

Purpose calls,

He says my name is Christ,

It is the second order,

It is called Christ and his Church,

Spirit for Spirit, Word for Word.


Purpose calls,

He says my name is Christ,

Chosen as the standard for the nation's of the earth,

The hands for the ingathering of the sons,

The form of the age, the depth of the age,

Fellowshipping in his presence as one.

Purpose calls,

He says my name is Christ,

Deep calling into Deep,

Predestined from the beginning of times,

Chosen for this life, equipped for the age,

The time is come.

Purpose calls.

# 2.
# In All Eternity

I already told the world of you.

For my mouth could not hold the words of you,

Words  you spoke to me.

My expressions could not hide you,

Because of its origin, it saw in you.

My thoughts experienced its nature,

Because it met you.

Your words, your expressions, your thoughts,

All love.


When you appear,

The world will tell you your stories;

For I made sure they heard,

They heard of you, every bit of you that I know.

From my words, my expressions, my thoughts

They saw, they saw you.

I love you.

So I say;

I will be loving you,

Till love says "I no longer exists".

But how can love no longer exist?

When you and I exist in all eternity..

# 3.

# My Truth

My heart is that of a ready writer,

Ready to spill,

Through my hands

Only that which it knows.

The heart knows it's truth,

You are my truth.


Truth;

you have shown me the path

I will never have found.

The tales of my life

Would have read "lost forever".

But your light ignited my heart,

And my heart caught it's unquenching fire.


Truth;

Now I'm on the path,

Burning with this fire that you started,

shining in you, with you, as you

On this path, that is life.

I'm truly living.

Truly, you are the truth.

I love you.

# 4.
# *Finding Him*

I sought him on the path of purpose,

When the night drew it's coverings on my path.

I knew He was the fulfillment

Of that which have been placed in my hands.

For my truth had told me He was the way,

Guiding me on the path, in the way to tread.


On I walked,

But my path only brought me fragrance of his presence.

No! not enough,

I wanted him;

For I wanted my mother's world to see him,

To see the tangibility of my truth I told them of,

To see the reality of my world within,

To have a taste of what life truly was.


I met the keepers of the path,

Asking, of the one I had come to love,

Asking, of the one who was the fulfillment

of that which was placed in my hands.

For I had come to understand in my walk,

That He was purpose himself.


It was night,

So the keepers took advantage of me;

How battered I was.

My heart did bleed;

From the whips of their armed mouth,

The arrows of their piercing words.

I screamed!!!

Yet, no battering was enough

To quench the fire of my passion,

To mellow the glow of my desire.

My mind was made,

I will find him whatever the cost.


After the keepers had left me,

Only a little had I gone by,

And there He stood in my very before.

I found him,

I found Christ.

# 5.
# *A Love Like Ours*

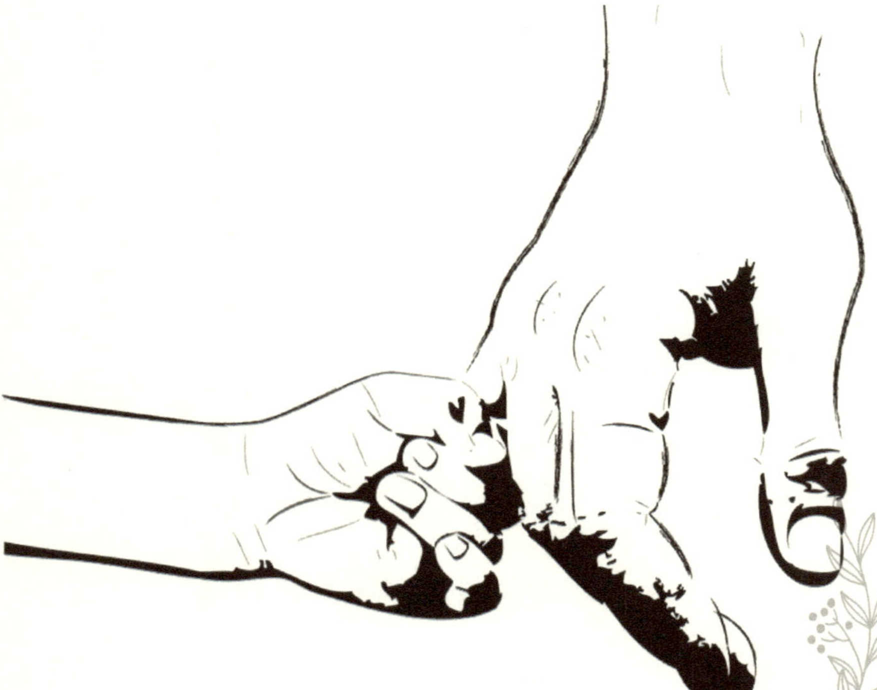

Who will believe my report?

I see you, in ways unusual

I hear you, in ways uncommon.

I already said yes,

But why do these figures still come by,

Demanding for my hand.

Do they not see the ring?

Or can't they remember

The day you came

That I was the bone taken from you

And now the flesh walking as you.


How will they see?

When the sky is the end they see

And pretend that beyond is their sight.

Anyway our love will burst,

Just from above the horizon;

So they could just, have a glimpse,

And see this love like ours

It has shown it's form in their sky sight.

Now they will better understand,

That a love like ours

Was always in existence;q

But only faith could hold.

# 6.
# The Perfect Church

Oh that I may attain self

Just as the scripture has shown,

That I may attain self

Just as my beloved sees,

And cover the distance that separates us.

Oh my beloved,

Take these foxes

That spoil the vineyards.

Take these foxes

That creates loopholes

For the vineyard is in bloom

And purpose extend its itching hands.


Oh that I may attain self,

Just as the scripture has shown;

The perfect church,

Living out my name;

Christ in me, I in Him;

Becoming one with my bethroted,

Fulfilling the father's plans.

Living out my truth;

This truth my reality,

My reality of identity,

The father's predestination.

The perfect Church,

Slowly dancing to the tunes of eternity,

My dance of mahanaim.

Oh how beautiful I dance,

Dancing between the worlds.

How did I get to this place?

That I must teach my young,

My young birthed in the spirit.

Purpose extending its itching hands

Purpose: - Christ.

Purpose: - The perfect Church.

# 7.
# Jeweled Shield

I want to wear my Jeweled Shield

The proof of my thousand victories,

The proof of my million victories.

How beautiful it would hang on my neck,

The display of my faith's fights,

And how much of a warrior I am.

Give me this battle and I will conquer;

The penetrating slice of my sword,

The word! the word!! The word!!!


I want to wear my Jeweled Shield

The proof of my thousand victories,

The proof of my million victories.

My lovers eyes,

As he beholds how beautiful I am,

And his mouth spills

The words he has patiently waited for this day to speak;

You are altogether beautiful my love,

See how you have led my young

And brought them to this place

And not one is missing.


Give me this battle and I will conquer,

So I could wear my Jeweled Shield.

The proof of my billion victories...

Oh how beautiful it would hang on my neck!

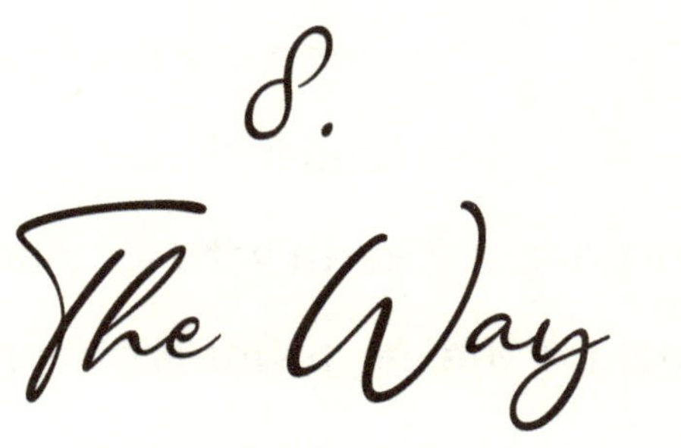

# 8.
# The Way

The world speaks

How loud it shouts;

Covering the earth with its shadows,

Feeding the earth with its fragment.

It tells the people;

The veil still exist.

Giving it's religion as the order of existence.

What bondage!

What lies!

That this world is all that exist,

That this world is in all the

Physicality the eyes can see,

That fulfillment is in all the money can buy,

That true success is at the cost of the soul.


My love is the fulfillment

My love is the true success

He is the only order for existence

Covering the earth with reality

Feeding the earth with fullness.

My Love is CHRIST!

# 9.
# Coming

Papa whispered into my ears,

He said you were coming,

How excited I was

I danced till I had no moves,

I sang till my voice was gone,

I wrote, yet my ink never running dry

because it was my special way

Of connecting to the love we shared;


I, writing the poems of my love

Which I would read out to you every day.

It was me talking to you from the depths of myself,

It was me saying the little the soul could express;

What it did feel for you.


Oh the news of your coming

gladdened my heart

I looked through the windows to the skies, to the streets,
to see if you were coming.

I put my ears by the door to know if I could hear your

footsteps,

If there would be a knock on the door.


Oh my love

How papa would laugh hard,

shaking his head as he watched me,

Prepare yourself he would say;

The feast is been prepared

Where you will dine as his one,

His stature fully grown into maturity.

Wait, Keep doing that which I have sent you.

# 10.
# The Love In His Love

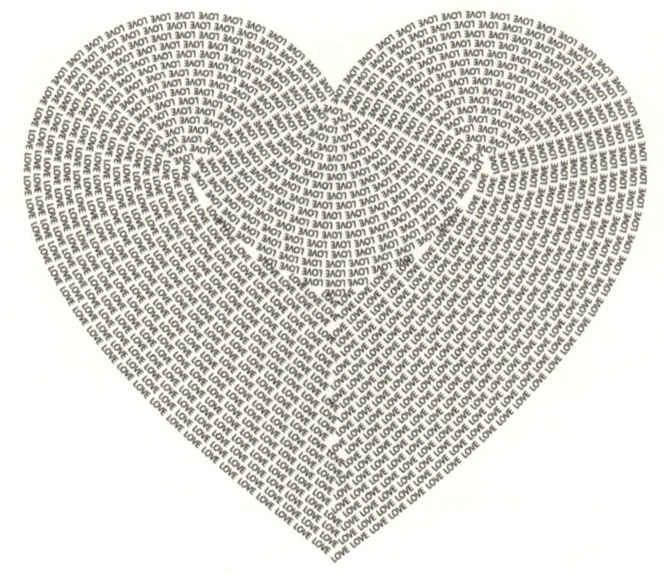

'The Love' of his will

Designed as a testament of 'His Love,'

A specie of his love.

His love the greatest of all.


'The Love' of his spirit

Birthed as a way of 'His Love,'

An original of his love.

His Love the greatest of all.


'The Love' of his soul

Entangled with the deepness of 'His Love,'

A depth of his love.

His love the greatest of all.


'The Love' of his body

The outstretched Hand of 'His Love,'

the tool of his love.

His love the greatest of all.

'The Love' of his presence

The flesh communicating 'His Love,'

The fullness of his love.

His love the greatest of all.

# 11.
# The Presence

Deep calleth unto deep,

Roaring deep calleth unto roaring deep.

Indeed only spirits whose depth

Has answered to the call

Knows how to find it.


This place of his presence

Where his divinity takes residence

We only but marvel

When our heart becomes the place of his presence.

Oh such beauty we display!


Oh master,

Yielded to you we are

Nothing of us in existence

Lost in the ambience of you

More, more, more our soul cries.

Oh master,

Take us till nothing is left of us

Our lives beholding your very being

Because you live through us

At your command we obey,

At your voice we tremble,

On your table we recline,

Feeding in fellowship

Operating from your realm.

# 12.
# My Home

I would never have thought

That life could be this perfect,

Till I found my home;

This place where I belong,

My Home, You.


I am overwhelmed!

What is this place,

That has found my deep

And fed my being;

Now I'm full of truth.

This place - My Home - You.


See me!

I can touch the clouds

and even beyond,

Because I'm truly living,

Living from this place.

This place made just for me.

This place - My Home - You.


My Home

Such Perfection of beauty,

Shining forth for this world to see.

# 13.
# I Will Fight

They want to take my future,

Never, I will fight.

For in those nights I dreamed those dreams

And saw those visions of spiritual elements,

Those visions with you, of us.

Yet they come with their pictures

Of artistry creations of physical elements,

Having manipulated in the spiritual.

Telling me that all I saw was a lie,

And my future did not exist.

Never, I will fight.


For it is written in the volume of books

I read of me,

Your vision shall be the world's reality,

As they smell the fragrance of my ability,

The power and influence

My existence holds in this territory.

I am, the one in charge

I am the church

and the truth which I bear

Must be made known.

This truth of love,

I will fight.

# 14.

## *The Name*

# CHRIST

I'm writing your name loud;

So that eyes can see your name bold.

For your name is what every man should know

And what this generation should hold.

It is a name like no other,

It is the shield invisible.


I want the world to know,

It is you I love.

How long can I hide

these convictions of mine

That wants to express itself?

It wants to tell the story,

The story of this name;

The name I will be expressing my life through,

In this territory of men.

Because this name has been named on me.

Predestination made its choice,

I, the one in whom the name was named on;

The name, Christ.

# 15.
# This Is Love

I will be loving you,

What joy!

Our love has no ending,

For nothing in existence

Can take you away from me,

We defeated death.

For death lost,

When we, walking past the fractions of time,

built our home,

Our home of eternity.

This is love,

The love with no end.

This is love,

The love with no separation,

For I am one body with this lord forever.

This is love,

The love with no pains,

Free from the cloak of uncertainties

For the future is already certain.

I am one,

One with you forever,

Ruling in you, with you, as you.

This is Love.

# 16.
# My Love

I want the world to know of

MY LOVE.

Know it deep,

That it is only you I see.

I'm taking every mountain,

So no one will say;

"I did not hear."

I'm expressing it with every action,

So no one will say;

"They did not see."

I'm living it with every consciousness,

So I will myself

Live my life in full.

My life the very expressions of you,

My life; your words alive,

Seen through me.

My world knowing my love,

My love is you

My love is only you.

Dear World,

Meet my love,

His name is CHRIST.

# 17.
# Love's Bowl

I found my way to the deep of love;

I saw the very source,

Where the love bow sprung from,

It was an everlasting sight.

It stood forth

All poured out,

Fulfilling all it's ever dreamt.

And in seconds,

I knew I was at the right place,

Cause only the right place knew this place,

You are my right place.


What is this?

This is love!

I found love's truth;

Love is pure, love is real,

Love is the only truth,

Enlightening to him who beholds,

Enchanting to him who resides,

Life to him who lives

Here; The right place.

You are my right place.

Love's Bowl.


My heart must express;

it has met it's finality,

No more searching,

No more allovers,

No more beginnings,

No more endings.

I'm alive, I'm alive

Here, Just Here

My right place,

Christ, you are my right place.

# 18.
# My Arrival

It was every day,

I took the only way

The distance seeming so unending,

The ending seeming never reaching.

My trust only in the words I heard,

When I chose this only path.


I saw the arrival of the many,

who chose the other way.

Their arrival seeming all glorious.

Time, time

Indeed was I slow or wrong

To have chosen this longer only way,

It was still the only way.


More time, more time,

Wait a minute,

The other way wasn't way at all,

Void of the price of fulfillment.

Within emptiness, outward happiness.

More time, more time

It was my arrival,

Having paid in full

The price of fulfillment;

Trust.

The tears danced it's version of joy,

Amidst the shouts of honour

And the inward comprehension;

That finally I arrived.

The time of the king church had come.

The other way certainly knew

The only way was the way.

The only way, CHRIST.

# 19.
# Manner Of Man

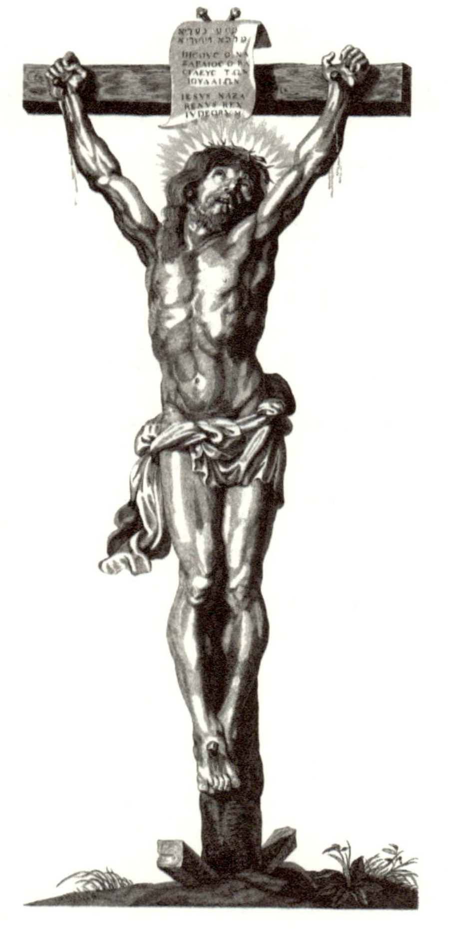

What manner of Man

The world wonders,

Your works still counting in the seen,

Yet the unseen breathes,

Breeds that which the world

Is yet to comprehend;

Because they could not read the spirit,

But only the letters of the Word.

They wonder,

Why they do what they do

But the prophecies of old

Must be made manifest.


Manner of Man

God in flesh made manifest,

It is you we follow,

Because we must feed to feed

Them who have been called,

Them who must not go missing,

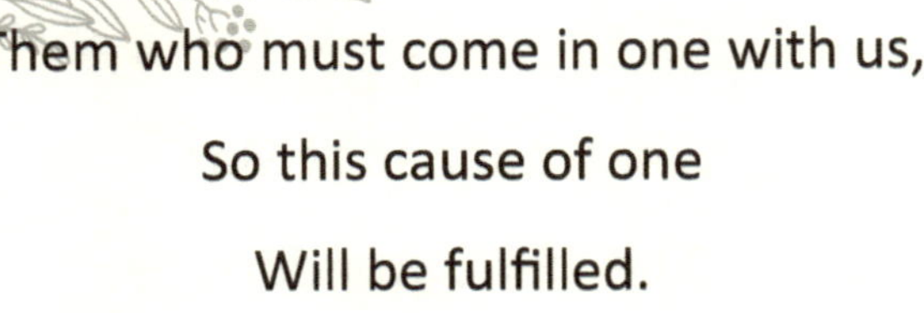

Them who must come in one with us,

So this cause of one

Will be fulfilled.


Manner of Man

Your days are here,

Your loins are filled,

Purpose fulfilled,

The heavens thunders

Manner of man.

# 20.
# Colours

I understood He had Colours,

Colours I had to let the world see.

Colours I had to give expressions to,

Cause the world needed him

To understand the shades of Colours it possessed.

The world needed to experience

his rain in colours

Living no place untouched,

The fullness of him,

Down poured in every place.


Rain, rain, rain

Colour of Holiness

Let the fragrance colours of peace be smelt,

the blowing-wind colours of  Life be embraced,

The tickling-drop colours of compassion be seen,

The cold-presence colours of truth be understood,

The ground-water full colours of love be enjoyed,

The resting Colours of healing be felt.

Colour, colours.

This colours I display

In my parade of living.

Truly, He is all the colours you need.

He is every shade,

He is CHRIST,

His colours I display.

# 21.
# My Deep Is You

My deep is you

You called me to my life,

You called me to my path,

You called me to truth,

You showed me the way;

It was the way you spoke,

My heart caught the fire,

Because somehow it knew you were different.


How could you know who I am?

My depth confirmed your precision

Of your knowledge of me.

Look at me;

I am free,

In this open place,

With my head high

running to fulfillment

Only because you called.

Gladdened I am,

Only because you came.

My deep is seen

Only because my deep is you.

# 22.
# I Saw Love

I saw love and love saw me.

"Isn't He beautiful?" was all I could say in my heart,

As my presence met his presence.

Melting in the Euphoria

Of the presence of my lord.

My presence humbly submitting

to the covering His presence brought.

My heart skipping in bits,

So it could blend

Into his skipping beating heart;

Perfect, one heart beating.


His words striking into my very depth,

Resounding the most powerful words

One, Is you and I

Spirit, word, flesh, bones.

Taking in deeper breaths,

Enjoying my relaxing depth

The depth that found it's truth in love,

Spoken with words,

Expressed in the spirit,

Now made flesh covering bones.

The beauty of been in love with love

I saw love and love saw me.

Christ is love in his church

Made flesh covering bones.

# 23.
# On That Day

On that day when my love shall appear;

I will shine brighter,

'Cause my world will see clearer,

I was indeed the light sent

to cause them to see in all this darkness.

The glory sent

to reveal his express image.

For every word I spoke of my love

Was the absolute truth.


He was the only way that was safe,

and the carbon way only took his form,

Portraying safety

but was death itself.


Look, look

Safety is only in my love.

My love, The Christ.

# 24.
# Love Of Faith

Love of faith!

Haven't you chosen my path,

What did you see

that you believe I will fulfill?

Love of faith!

Let me tell you my story;

the ground has in its several

had a taste of my back.

Long I stayed, yet somehow

did my feet stand the ground.


"Love of faith"

Why do you bring me another mystery?

"The bed of green"

A bed I must share with another,

A bed where all the young will lay

and rise to fulfill their morning bidding.

"Love of faith"

You are sure he will appear

and take hold of this awaiting hands

and together we lay the bed of green,

Fulfilling the time.


Love of faith

Your journey have I taken,

my trust in all you said

and all you have shown.

Our bed is green.

At last in this place will I build.

# 25.
# Those Nights

It is one of those nights again

When my heart revels  the presence of you,

Just listening to hear the penetrating sound

Of your voice that bears the words,

The keeps my lamp burning

and my cup full of its extra oil.

Reveling the echoing sound of laughter

Emanating from your depth

Because of the wisdom we share.


I must say, I am brave.

Brave to have the heart that burns for you,

The mouth that speaks of you,

The life that lives in your love,

Even before your appearance

To affirm my heart is right,

My words are true,

and My life is truth.


Anyway the truth is the truth,

Our love exists.

What history it will make

In these times that come,

Because everyone will see

Nothing hidden, when you appear,

the fruits of what we share;

Pure, perfect

Our love.

# 26.
# *Your Heart*

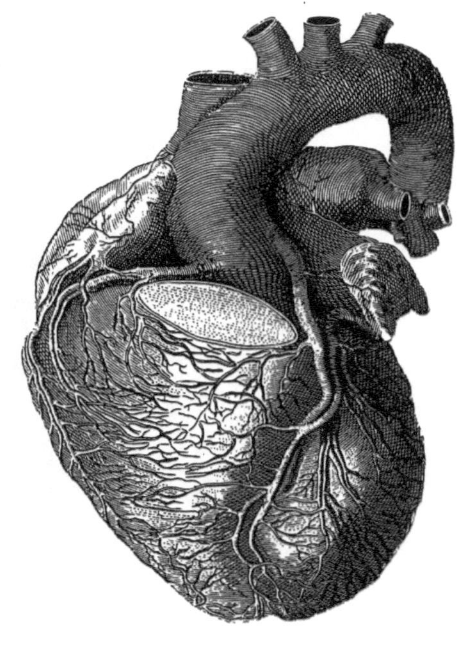

I will show the world your heart

So they could see the truth,

The truth of who you are.

Coming to their enlightenment,

They will see you are innocent

Guiltless of all the charges,

Their submissions have charged you with.

You gave them all,

And never have you held anything back.


I will show them your heart

So they could comprehend your love.

It's depths

And the electrifying power of your compassion

for one as single as one.

Your desire to be with one

More than their cravings could afford.

You gave a love,

That cost such price.

See your heart,

Love most powerful

All in existence.

# 27.
# *Portrait Of My Forever*

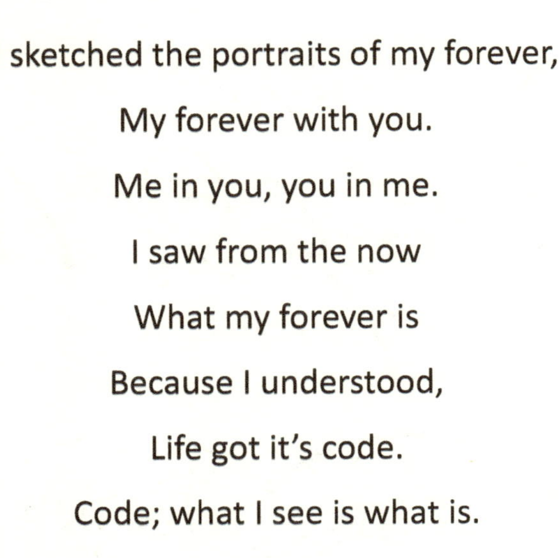

I sketched the portraits of my forever,

My forever with you.

Me in you, you in me.

I saw from the now

What my forever is

Because I understood,

Life got it's code.

Code; what I see is what is.

Code; what I say is what is.


I sketched the portraits of my forever,

Seeing the truth,

One flesh with you;

On a course that had a name,

On a path well defined,

In a way that was an only.

Predestination had made its choice.

This portrait hanging on the

walls of all times.

Everyone who lives will see

This portrait of the forever.

# 28.
# I Will Write You

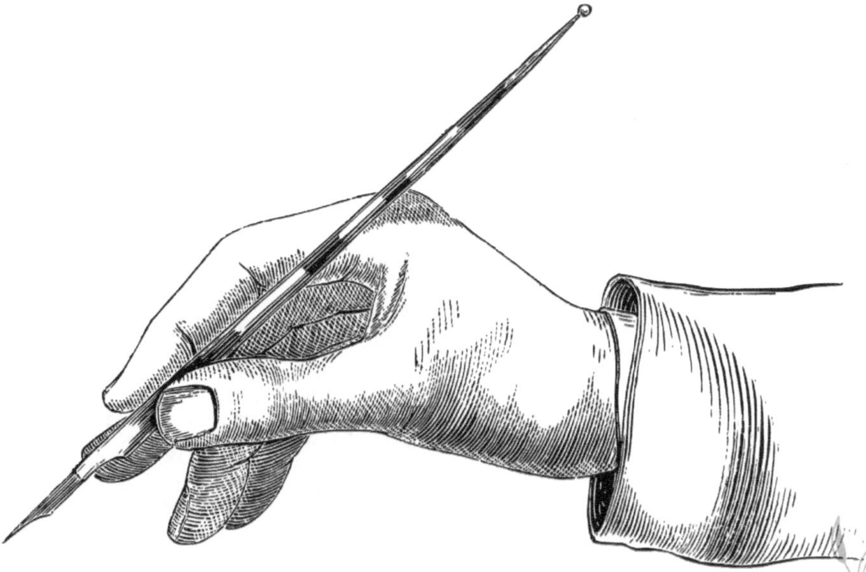

I will write you

Till the world reads you from me,

In the book of you written by me.

It will contain the pages of all your inscriptions

My writings have been able to decode

From my heart processing,

after taking my cue from the word

You already have given.

It would tell how

Powerfully beautiful the world in you is,

Communicating the fullness of your depths

The world should have a glimpse of.


I will write you

till the world understand the truth,

The truth of this identity;

You are love.

# 29.
# In The Beginning

Creation why didn't you tell me,

Why did you hide this from me?

Why didn't you tell me from my beginning?

Love saw me at my birth,

When my form came to being.

How did love know

That I was who I am?

How did love code my coding designs,

Raveling the imprints of my existence

Playing the truth strings of  me

With such exact mode.

Love was certainly in the beginning.


Creation,

You should have told me,

So this poor mind

Wouldn't logically express self.

It would have understood

Faith was the realm to express self.

In faith, Love's work is done

My being is exposed to self,

My being is expressing depth,

My song, most expressively chanting:

I'm living, living, living everyday.

Only love could know this much,

Love was certainly in the beginning.


Creation you did tell me,

How loudly you told!

Expressing very explicitly, with nothing hidden from me,

Witnessing ever profoundly from the beginning.

Only I, just saw.

How couldn't love have known all me.

Love was in the beginning.

# 30.
# Faith

I was given faith

down the pathway of life.

She was a baby placed in my hands.

I saw a note

Just by her carrier.

It read

"Her name is faith,

She has been placed in your hands

She is to be fed, weaned and must grow.

Her growth depends on your care,

She is a different kind of child,

She would never grow without your attention,

Your attention is the trust on instructions.

Years might run in numbers

Yet a baby she would remain

If your love is not in action,

pushing beyond what is seen".


Indeed baby faith was a handful.

I cared with the word

Seeing her eyes open

Each time her face attempted to smile.

Then it was the little baby steps.

Time, time, time

And she was a young child

Running all over the place.

Years where spent beyond the normal

For her to be the young child.

Times, lost I my care

Times, failed I to trust

There sat her in tears,

Her growth now impossible

Cause nothing could feed her.

Somehow she understood the unusual

and wouldn't feed.

How she would spring up

Each time my trust in instructions gained it's weight

Feeding fat from my care,

Her growth now possible.

Here she is with me

A little grown over ten,

Time spent some money

On getting her here.

Yet my excitement knows beyond

Because it sees

The beauty she would possess

As a young woman.

The perfection of beauty.

# 31.
# I Will Wait

I will wait

Because you said.

When my yearnings search for words

From the outer space

To make me feel love.

Yet, your word will be the inner space

My yearnings will search through.

It would read from your songs,

Your songs of love to me.

This lyrics says;

"Beautiful you are,

How captivating are your eyes".


I will wait

Because you said.

When my hold desires a heart.

Yet, my hold will choose one heart,

Yours of course.

Seeing as you see,

Loving as you love.

Lost in the embrace of oneness with you,

Your presence is the everything.


I will wait

Because you said

My depth has found its truth

The long-suffering paid this price.

Gold I am.

The quest to own me has began.

Attention!!

This gold is already owned.

I will wait

Because you said.

# 32.
# Bond

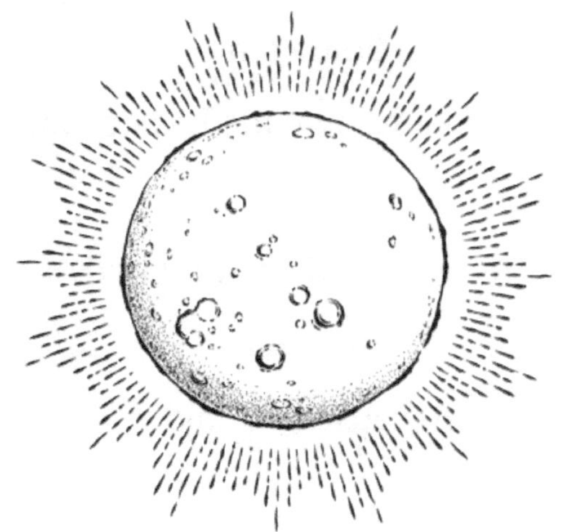

Night, Night

What is the name of that star

Twinkling through this night?

I named it.


For in all those times faith had to speak,

and I had to wait.

The night had to reveal

the knowledge of this love,

So my day could utter

The understanding of the love.


Shinning through the galaxy you stood,

Let me shine this much you spoke,

Lightning with your sparkling smile.

Your presence was felt,

Making stay every memory in the wait.


Night, night,

"Bond" have I named that star.

The memories;

Life's reminder that I met love when it was dark.

Yet, Chose he my hands to hold,

Chose he my heart to own,

Chose he my life to live.


Day, Day

The bond began in that night

When love revealed itself,

And all I do in your time is speak

Of the bond love and I share.

Named I that star;

Bond.

You shined through the night.

# 33.
# Well Of Love

Well of love,

Everyday I draw.

Now I am an ocean full and ever flowing.

See the people!

roundly all gathered,

Wanting the draw from me.

I'm enough, I'm enough

Filling every gathered to an overflowing.


Well of love,

In this day found I you,

When the dryness took every strength

Leaving me empty full.

Living waters was it,

That filled the chambers of my belly

and flowed to my flesh.

I'm full, I'm full

Overflowing in my within.


Well of love,

I took the draw.

I must confess,

This draw is life.

The ocean of life.

# 34.
# All Shades Of You

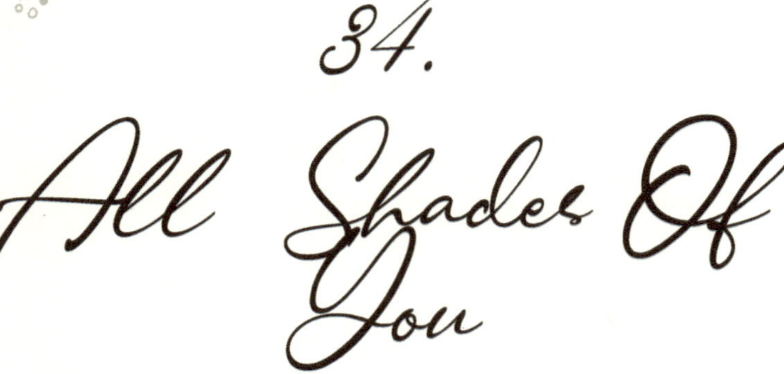

If I could be all shades of you,

I will shine till darkness loses its face.

Taking every kingdom till every kingdom has your name

Winning every heart till every heart knows your
presence

Speaking forth your name till your name is seen all over.

That the world's whole may know you

That the world's whole may see you

That the world's whole may understand that life begins
and ends with you.


If I could be all shades of you

I will shine till the whole world sees your light

The light you made of me,

The truth you made of my existence

Nothing else matters, matters without you

You are the foundation of all existence

You are God, the God of lights,

Making mysteries, revealing mysteries

Every man's truth, Every man's depth

Every man's freedom, freedom to truly living.


If I could be all shades of you,

I will shine till everyone knows you are light,

You are the only way,

You are the only truth,

You are the only life,

Beautiful to understand

Christ has made me all shades of you.

# 35.
# Everyday

Love, this heart reaches out

Craving in silence your knowledge;

The yearnings of your heart

The understanding of your thoughts.

Your ways it wants to follow

Expressing its being exactly as you.

Everyday, living for you.


Love, this heart deep

Craving your feet to sit by,

Lying always some distance not too far

Beholding your face and hearing the

Drips from your mouth;

They are as honey

From the jar of the father's comb

Bursting forth like waters

Filling every place.

I'm filled, overflowing.

Everyday, living for you

Love, more, more

My cravings desires.

Everyday, perfectly living for you.

# 36.
# *Journey*

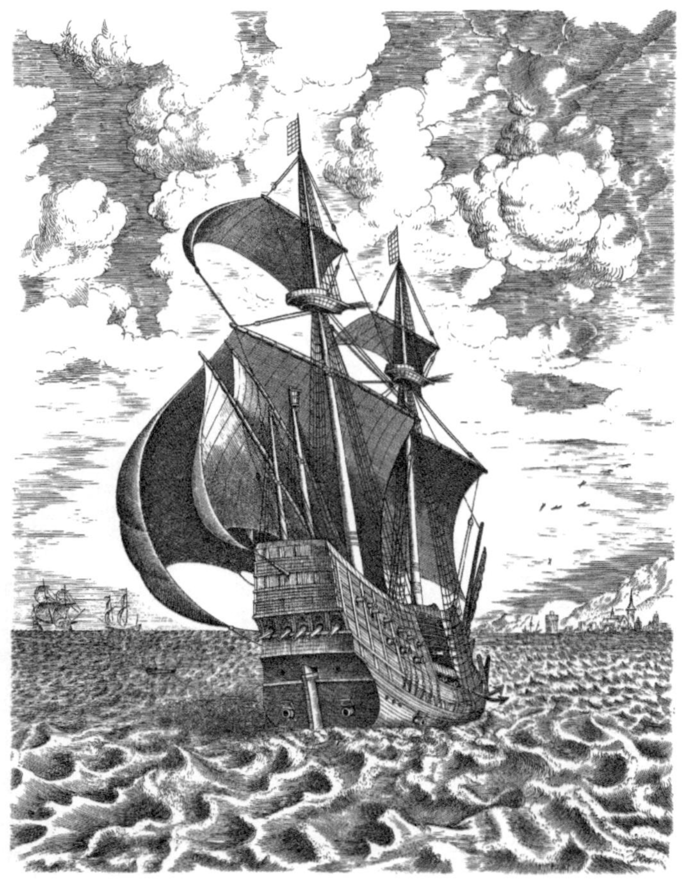

Finding love wasn't a quest

Self would ever have thought of journeying on.

Taking each turns, the aching desire

To fulfill something with a name,

To attain best.

Stories, stories I heard of that man

He seemed to be this much

Having a unique ability to fly the seasons

And supernaturally understand every path.

I met him,

First he was to me all that I heard

Nothing of my unique personal knowledge.

I learnt the chant they usually sang him,

They say

"It could trigger his action part".

Chant 1; I love you

Chant 2; I thank you

Chant 3; I praise you.

Sure didn't mean anything to me.

My mouth speaking in deceit

What wasn't in my heart.

Then I met him,

It was a big wild fall.

How could I hide?

Everyone was bound to see,

My name would hang finally

In the walls of shame.

Shame would be the new name

Because the stigma

Would always refer me as her course.


Wait a minute they didn't see!

No one saw?

It was evident.

It was him;

His cloud blinded their eyes,

His hands gave me my lifting,

His words showed me the way.

Now I'm fulfilling something with a name,

His name.

And never have I heard a word of the fall,

It never happened.

This is love.

Now I'm on this journey with him,

He found me, now I have found him.

I must say, Love took the journey himself

Never ever has he left my side.

Now my chant meaning every letter.

I love you.

# 37.
# Who Has Seen Love

Who has seen love?

Let him speak at night.

So the heart who wonders

In search of the deep,

May hear the words

And find his way to love bow.

For only the night sheweth the knowledge.


Who has seen love?

Let him speak,

There will always be one to learn.

For The one who wonders

Will feed his deep with all

the night has shown.

Waiting for the day to appear

To run his speech.

Speaking forth the truth,

And living out all of he has seen.

Just as the day expressing

and speaking with its clouds

all it had heard at night.


Who has seen love?

Let him speak.

# 38.
## Search

Deep will search,

Search for every word it needs

To describe the depth it understands.


Can you see?

It's The faith of my love;

You are real and your warming presence

Is where I live.


Can you feel?

It's the strength of my love;

In you I am the government ruling in this space

Showing forth the only truth.


Can you hear?

It's the words of my love

I'm same with you, one in and as you

Framing the world's as it ought to be.

Can you smell?

It's the fragrance of my love

I'm taking your presence to every world

In demonstration of who you are in me..


Can you taste?

It is the desire for my love

More, more because knowing you

Is in dimensions that keeps unfolding.

I got it,

But wait a minute there is still more.

Deep search

Let love know

Deep  search

Let love know I have understood

I am the expression.

# 39.
# Fruits Of The Spirit

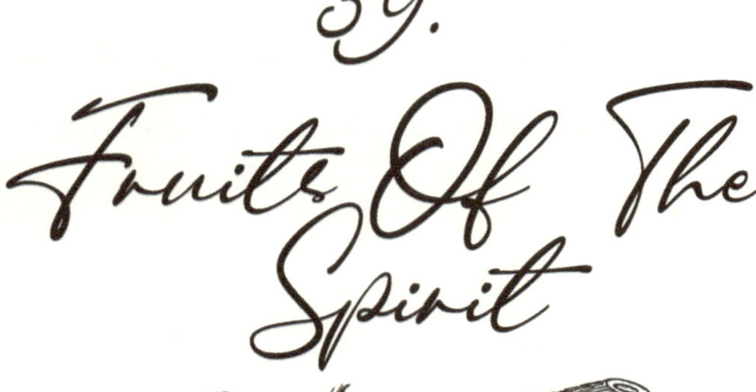

I have learnt the way of life

These fruits are my evidence.

Patience bought me a seat,

While self control kept me from standing.

I saw the love expressions of you,

For it taught me the healing powers of kindness.

The gentling presence of you

gifting me with the best of peace.

In faithfulness i have

birthed my son of joy

Filling my world with all your goodness.

Now, Humility have lifted me from the seat

Showing my fruits to all the world,

"Eat it" declares, for pure is this.

Overflowing with every grace

This way of life was taught

Only by your spirit.

I have learnt the way of life,

These fruits are my evidence.

# 40.
# Holy City

O Holy city,

What memories you bring me,

Your love totally expressed

You show me.

The place you paid for me,

The place you gave all for me,

The place you saw just me.

O holy city,

The night of my engagement

When you took the debts

And nailed to the cross.

You paid the world so you could own me.


O Holy city,

What memories you bring me,

The path you chose,

The life you gave me,

Your spirit the seal

That the world is the least in all I own.

O Holy city

What memories you bring me,

I saw your eyes the night,

I heard your words

You looked in me,

You saw what I could not see.

Church you crowned me,

Your body you called me.

Christ you are to me.

O Holy city

What memories you bring me.

# 41.
# Fat With Feed

Have I not said the way it is

This truth that I know;

It is you.

You have awoke me from the sleeping sleep

that got drunk my existence,

Keeping me cold on the sail.

Extracting as wick,

You have set me burning,

Keeping me in weather.


This is the cause we must follow,

You feed me fat

For all that is ahead.

How do you do?

Is a code existence would never understand doesn't
exist.

I'm fat with feed

Enough to satisfy every drought,

Full to fill every emptiness,

Overflowing to make wet every dryness.

Back to sail,

I'm fat with feed

To silence every storm,

Rolling through every wave,

Feeding all who are on ship,

Saving them who are drowning.

You have fed me fat.

# 42.
# The Deep

This deep is calling; won't you answer?

The way is one; won't you follow?

The life is one;won't you live?

The deep roars

Who can hear?

The deep roars

Won't you but listen?

Time is not all,

Time is but the fraction

Eternity is the whole but only in one.

One, The Christ.

There is an open space

With no fraction to bind,

Just the whole to explore.

Yet ,your choice is the gateway to access.

What would it be

To the deep that roars inside of you?

The fraction is short

Ticking away it's life;

Tick, tock, tick, tock.

The deep roars,

The way is now open, take it.

For eternity soon draws,

Its curtain close on this way.

# 43.
# Faith Was Wounded

My little child faith, was wounded,

I stood in tears unmoving

watching her bleed so profusely.

Pain immediately went for my heart,

Digging, digging

Till there was a hole.


My heart asked,

what will happen?

The body answered;

"Leave her to die,

I told you from times beginning

She was never worth it.

Your patience in growing her

Into the young woman

you try to create in your heart

Will never work."

The Spirit answered with questions

"What have you heard?

Who did the words come from?

What was said about this child?

In the old, what wonders have this child done?

what has she brought your way?

She is a little grown over ten,

You watched her as a baby

Her first steps,

Then she was running,

A little over five she became,

Now she is a little over ten.

I ask again, what would it be."

Taking in breaths,

lost in thought, one choice will be made.

The pictures make their way

Through my heart,

The pictures of what she had done

And the ones I had created of what

Her journey on becoming a

Young woman would be.

I made my way to her,

Faith my love child.

Picking her up, cleaning her wounds

the hole in my heart disappeared.


Yet, the scars are there,

a reminder of faiths journey,

She is beautiful.

The joy that fills my heart

As I watch her grow.

# 44.
# I'm In Love

Into my deepest you call,

Into my deepest you see,

Into my very existence you made,

My spirit being and yours are one.

Because we fellowship,

Rubbing off substances.

into my eyes you look,

The smile on my face you behold,

The peace in my being you gave,

This heart of mine, an offering it became

Just because its the way you want to see it

Just because its the way you  made it.


I'm in love, I'm in Love

But this time is with you

Deep calleth unto deep

Your voice resounding in my soul

Your presence mesmerising my entire being

You have become a Friend,

You have become a Father,

You have become a Lover,

The Inspiration.


For honour you have chosen this vessel,

The creator which holdeth the universe,

The potter which holdeth the clay

The master whom adopted the slave

You have lifted the one with the pen.

The deep has called.

# 45.
# Shoe Size

What is my shoe size

I asked this purpose of mine?

Too big is this,

It won't fit so well.

How often I would fall,

The Joker of my time I would be,

Giving everyone the laugh of life.


No, then self have you not understood,

This purpose of mine said;

For the word has given this to you,

So perfectly, this will fit.

Expressing the one  you are,

No fall can cause your fall

Cause word-process has grown your feet,

Gave it strength,

And chose the path this shoe can tread.

For what The Word has called,

That is what it is.

The infleunce of your time would you be,

Giving everyone the life that is truth.

This size knows only your feet.

Too perfect is this.

Here is your shoe size.

# 46.
# Papa's Dream

Dreamy, this night is cold

What will keep me warming hot

Till this night is past,

Rolling its pillows away.

Warming hot Papa's memories in display,

And  I, sharing in moments those memories.

Wide awake, the optical has just seen

It's most beautiful,

How powerful I felt.

Memories in display,

Memories of me

I had already lived.

Living the life my present always desired.

The dream,

Papa's dream all in full bloom.


Wow,

The night already warming hot,

I found my mouth.

Papa, that is me.

Everything I did, all in the way you desired,

Fulfilling you.

Replied him me,

"Memories, memories

Your future are my memories,

Trust the me at work in you.

You are the dream,

You are Papa's dream already fulfilled,

The full bloom."

# 47.
# Soul

Dear souls,

Hear I your calls,

Seeing the ties that clings strongly to your neck,

the feast with struggles,

Searching for the way not to dine.

The bird wish,

Wings on me so i could fly

Soaring high in the skies.

In this open air

When the wind blows touching my every part.

Playing its calming sounds

Bringing  the freshness of all it carries.

Just to be without

this weight, this existence brings

Free, free.

What is this way out,

Way would you show me,

This lost wants to be found.

I am that which gives the freedom that you have

For the beginning knows I'm it's beginning,

Owing the right to ending.

Codes, I made every,

Existence is just one, the weight is nothing.

I see even the unseen,

I am the way out.

I am the freedom that you seek

I am the WORD.

The Word who is LOVE.

# 48.
# You Were There

How time tries to cover

With its leaves of distance

The path we once treaded together.

The trees on this part

With their everyday fruiting fallings,

Tries to erase the memories

With the wealth of fruits all laid.

No day an escape.


Yet no one chews,

Because no one can see these fruits,

Just you and I.

So I'm going to chew as much,

Rid these paths of these leaves as much,

Because these memories of us

are footprints I want to see every time.

It reminds me of how

My journey of perfection began,

You were there

And you held my hands.

# 49.
# Loving You

Loving you was the extra oil

That kept my lamp burning.

Burning for the world to see its light,

Know its truth.

Outshining every darkness,

No matter its weight.

See the lies,

Finding every corner to hide its shame.


Loving you was the path

I had taken in the way.

A path I will walk in every day

It gave the definition of me.

How would I have known

What I was all about.

You are Church.


Loving you was the mystery revealed,

The purpose understood,

The supernatural unfolded,

The identity embraced.

His perfect church: Christ.

Loving you is my life expressed,

Loving you.

# 50.
# Echoes Of Depth

What world you have created

Scintillating to the darkness of them

Who sail on the surface.

In hope,

Someday they could sail in the deep,

Seeing the world that was created.

It is Beyond that which they could think to seek,

Carrying the most precious,

Made for every, all one.

It had a price

Yet, only love's blood could afford.

Love died.


Echoes of depth

Will you resound in their deep

The truth of all that love did.

Disfigured beyond recognition,

Naked walking down the streets to golgotha.

It paid off,

The veil that kept this world from its creator

Was torn.

Will you just see

What love has done and embrace all it has given.

For "soon" is the number of  time

that will close this way,

No Daysman shall stand by

When eternity ticks on time clock.

The world love created

will be for them who embraced deep.

After all, Love did it all, even for them

Who were on stay on the surface.


Echoes play this tunes of depth

Love gave the complete package.

Ageless even when the number of years add by,

Oneness with the essence of love himself,

Health in the flesh that carries you.

What a way to live.

All this world that love created.

It is love all the way.

Echoes of depth.

# Prayer Of Salvation

(Kindly pray this prayer, and mean it with all your heart).


Oh Lord God,

Believing has become my reality,

For my heart has understood

The son of the one living God is Jesus.

He did die, defeating death;

He stood raised, Now alive!

Lord God,

This choice have I made

And my mouth bears this confession;

Jesus is lord of my life this day,

Life eternal I now have,

Through him and in his name.

Again have I been born.

Thank you, for your choice of me

Has saved my soul.

A child of yours am I now.

Hallelujah is my new song.

Precious Ozeme